EGYPT

ANTIQUITIES FROM ABOVE

EGYPT

ANTIQUITIES FROM ABOVE

MARILYN BRIDGES

ESSAY BY PENELOPE LIVELY

A BULFINCH PRESS BOOK LITTLE BROWN AND COMPANY BOSTON • NEW YORK • TORONTO • LONDON

Captions by Thomas Bridges

First edition

Library of Congress Cataloging-in-Publication Data
Bridges, Marilyn.
Egypt : antiquities from above / Marilyn Bridges ; essay by Penelope Lively.
p. cm.
"A Bulfinch Press book."
ISBN 0-8212-2257-0 (hc)
1. Egypt — Antiquities. 2. Egypt — Antiquities — Aerial photographs. 3. Egypt — Aerial photographs. I. Title.
DT60.B747 1996
932 — dc20 96-33937

Designed by Germaine Clair
Printed by Hull Printing Company
Bound by Acme Book Binding

Bulfinch Press is an imprint and trademark of Little, Brown and Company (Inc.)
Published simultaneously in Canada by Little, Brown & Company (Canada) Limited

PRINTED IN THE UNITED STATES OF AMERICA

Frontispiece:
Great Temple of Ramesses II and Lake Nasser, Abu Simbel, 1993

CONTENTS

TO THE PEOPLE OF EGYPT, WHOSE ANCESTORS CREATED THESE WONDROUS MONUMENTS.

ACKNOWLEDGMENTS

A heartfelt thanks to everyone who helped make this book possible, especially:

My Egyptian friends for their generous support, particularly Dr. A. A. Abdullah and Captain Yahia El Agaty;

The Egyptian Ministry of Defense for allowing me to fly over restricted territory and the Egyptian Air Force for providing me with extremely proficient pilots;

Dr. Dieter Arnold and Dr. Dorothea Arnold, of the Department of Egyptian Art at the Metropolitan Museum of Art, whose expertise was invaluable;

My ground support at home, Felicia Murray, Tom Bridges, and David Blust;

Janet Bush, who, as my editor, believed in this project from the start;

And to my mother, Elizabeth Davis, 1916–1995, who gave me the tenacity to pursue my dreams.

— MARILYN BRIDGES

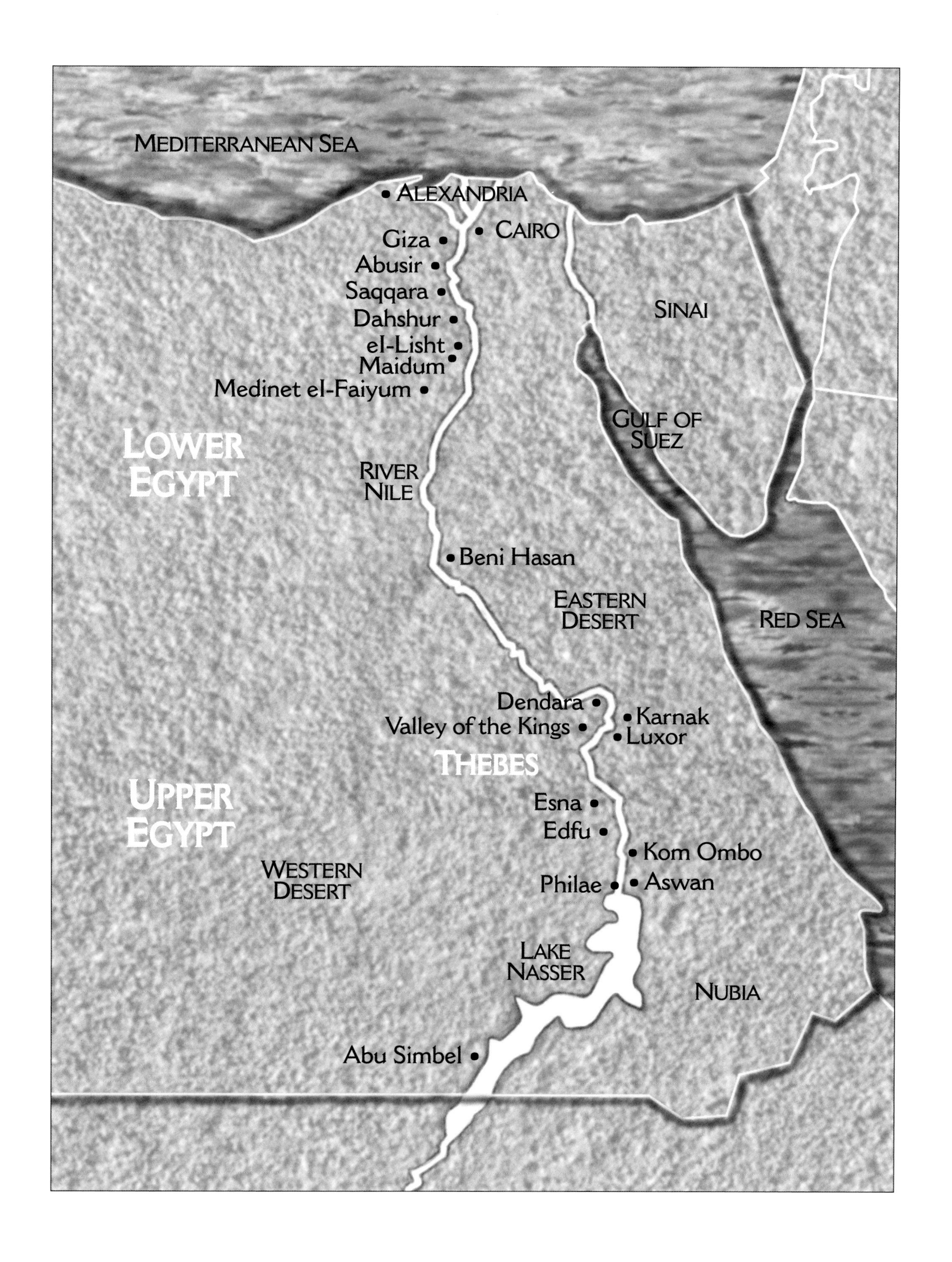
MEDITERRANEAN SEA
ALEXANDRIA
CAIRO
Giza
Abusir
Saqqara
Dahshur
el-Lisht
Maidum
Medinet el-Faiyum
SINAI
GULF OF SUEZ
LOWER EGYPT
RIVER NILE
Beni Hasan
EASTERN DESERT
RED SEA
Dendara
Karnak
Valley of the Kings
Luxor
THEBES
UPPER EGYPT
Esna
Edfu
Kom Ombo
WESTERN DESERT
Philae
Aswan
LAKE NASSER
NUBIA
Abu Simbel

THREE PYRAMIDS OF GIZA WITH CAIRO, 1993

A Glimpse of Time

Penelope Lively

A visit to the Nile valley wonderfully concentrates the mind. The great monuments — the pyramids, the temples, the tombs — put the onlooker neatly in perspective. You feel diminished, in every sense — by the sheer weight of all that stone, and by the implications of those great reaches of time. A single life is neither here nor there, before the eternal gaze of the figures at Abu Simbel, or alongside the brilliant continuing daily life of the tomb paintings. Marilyn Bridges's fine photographs extend this vision by whirling the spectator up to see the monuments from a point of view that diminishes humanity almost to extinction. The Luxor temples appear as carven permanences with an attendance of human figures like a scatter of ants. A godlike finger could stub them out, you feel.

There is a nice anachronism here. This is one of the most populous areas of the world — a strip of soil that is intensely fertile, thanks to the benevolent silt borne down annually by the Nile floods, and that has sustained human life since the most distant periods of prehistory. There has been more concentrated human existence here than perhaps anywhere else, and the calm, almost inhuman survival of the monuments is an anachronistic testimony to the passage of so many lives. These edifices were built by people — a hundred thousand or so in the case of the Great Pyramid, sweating, striving, exhausted men hauling those great blocks up from the banks of the Nile. And, thinking this, you suddenly cease to see the place in terms of kings and gods and think of that teeming infrastructure of men, women, and children whose descendants are still there, many of them doing much the same as their distant ancestors, reaping a living from that rich deposit of mud.

I grew up in that landscape, a few miles outside Cairo, and when I conjure it up today in the mind's eye, it is as a scene of bustling activity. The fields of sugarcane or of berseem (a kind of clover mainly used as animal fodder) were busy with people — men and women bent double over their work, children leading a column of camels or driving a donkey so laden that it appeared as four hooves tittupping below a great mound of cane or greenstuff. It was like a medieval landscape, the visual manifestation of an agricultural economy dependent upon intensive labor and quite unfamiliar to any Westerner for whom agriculture means a tractor creeping across an empty field. When first I came to England as an adolescent, I looked with astonishment at the deserted fields and lanes of Somerset — where was everyone?

Life has been short, alongside the Nile. When I was a child, the expectation of life of the Egyptian peasant was around forty — not much changed, I should imagine, from the expectations of the ancient world. Poverty and disease are endemic. The waters of the Nile, which bestow life, also erode it by acting as harborer of the snails that carry bilharzia, the deadly debilitating disease that attacks so many fellahin — though today that particular curse is in retreat, thanks to stringent efforts to eradicate the snail breeding grounds. So too is trachoma, the eye affliction that has traditionally caused a high level of blindness. Returning to Egypt today, I see people who look more robust, less diseased, children who are larger and healthier. Ironically, they look more like the figures of the tomb paintings, those elegant and assured folk of Pharaonic times, forever intent upon their fishing, their hunting, their netting of wildfowl, and their propitiation of the gods, those volatile autocrats who might at any moment inflict death and disaster upon all or any.

Mortality is the theme of the Nile Valley. The great monuments are statements of defiance — the attempts of kings and queens to surmount the human condition. And in a curious way they do indeed succeed. The name of Ramesses lives on — even if ignominiously attached to that of the Cairo Hilton. Tens of thousands of tourists from all over the world struggle to pronounce the name of Queen Hatshepsut as they gaze upon her temple on the west bank at Thebes. The religion of ancient Egypt was devoted to the idea of provid-

Great Sphinx from the South, Giza, 1993

ing for the soul in the afterlife — a tacit denial of the unacceptable. Life was brief, death was all around — so in defiance you made certain that your soul and those of your ancestors were provided with all the goods needed for the maintenance of life: the food and drink, the comforts and possessions. And if you were in the happy position of being able to call upon the inexhaustible supplies of labor, you built a pyramid or a temple to your own eternal glory.

We walk today amid that glory, in the Nile Valley — or fly above it. The landscape of today is a temporal kaleidoscope, with everything coexisting — the pyramids and the temples and the tombs alongside the ruins left by the Romans and the Greeks, the mosques of the Mamluks, the surviving shreds of eighteenth- and nineteenth-century Cairo. A temple sits comfortably alongside a contemporary brickworks, a medieval mosque rises from the clutter of a modern slum. Marilyn Bridges's photograph of Luxor shows the temple like some stately ship moored beside the jumble of today's town. The past is always within sight — you stub your toe on it, walk around a corner slap into it, finding it looming above you. The whole country is like some vast casual rubbish heap — turn over the sand or the soil and there are the potsherds, the coins, the beads, all the silent but eloquent evidence that a great many people have been here before.

When I was very young — six or seven, maybe — I was taken for a special trip into the desert. We were going to see some people digging, I was vaguely told. I remember standing in the buff wastes of the dunes and staring down at a round shallow depression in which lay the delicate outline of a skeleton, like a pattern blown upon the sand — the serrations of the ribs, the fine fan of the hand. And it came to me that this was a person — had once been a person who had walked and breathed here just as I did now. I caught a glimpse of time, and of mortality. I now know that what I saw must have been a pre-dynastic burial — my memory of a figure crouched in a natal position accords precisely with descriptions of those very early prehistoric burial sites, those of some of the earliest inhabitants of the Nile Valley. It was a seminal moment for me and has stayed with me all my life, impressing me far more than the familiar pyramids and the Sphinx, which we visited frequently. Everyone had pyramids, didn't they?

I suppose the powerful impact of that burial was because of the perception of shared humanity and also of immensities of time — of a long ago much more distant than the childish vision of last week or last month. Growing up with pyramids did not have quite the same effect, or at least not at the time. I am one of millions of Nile-nurtured children for whom a daily view of antiquity is nothing to wonder at but simply a part of the scenery. In the last century, before the temples were excavated, this cohabitation must have been even more pronounced. Lucie Duff Gordon, the early Victorian traveler who came to Egypt in an attempt to cure her consumption, lived in a house built on top of the Temple of Luxor, which was still buried in the sandy soil. Gustave Flaubert described the scene a little later, in 1850: "[Luxor] can be divided into two parts, separated by the two pylons: the modern part, to the left, contains nothing old, whereas on the right the houses are on, in, or attached to the ruins. The houses are built among the capitals of the columns: chickens and pigeons perch and nest in the great [stone] lotus leaves; walls of bare brick or mud form the divisions between houses; dogs run barking along the walls. So stirs a mini-life amid the debris of a life that was far grander. . . ." Visitors of today can see the graffiti scored by nineteenth-century tourists onto the very tops of the pillars of the Karnak temple, which only protruded a few feet then. They walked above our heads, as it were — a dizzying inversion of time and space that reinforces the Nile Valley's rejection of conventional notions of chronology.

Lucie Duff Gordon is perhaps the most attractive of the nineteenth-century European Nile visitors, on account of her own courage in the face of illness and isolation from her family, but also for the sympathetic interest she took in the society that she found. She became a beloved figure in Luxor, and her *Letters from Egypt* should be read by anyone who makes that journey upriver today. The antiquities themselves rather left her cold — people were her passion. Amelia Edwards is of a different order. She was the quintessential amateur Egyptologist of the late Victorian period, a formidable lady who hired her own crew to get herself up to Abu Simbel, where she set her crew to cleaning off the heads of the statues — then still up to their necks in sand — with sponges and tinting the exposed stone with coffee for greater aesthetic effect.

Amelia Edwards is a product of the mania for Egyptian antiquities that began in the Napoleonic era and gathered momentum throughout the nineteenth century, culminating in the frenzy over the discovery of the tomb of Tut'ankhamun in the 1930s. During this hundred years and more, the place was pillaged by European collectors, with the assistance of professional tomb robbers who had been breaking into the tombs for thousands of years and the active connivance of the Turkish administration, which profited nicely. It is no wonder that the museums of the world are stuffed with ancient Egyptian artifacts, and also that the characteristic style of ancient Egyptian art has become an image familiar throughout the world, detached from its origins and woven into the fabric of interior decor and of architectural fashion.

In 1849 Gustave Flaubert climbed the Great Pyramid. "The stones, which at a distance of two hundred paces seem the size of paving-blocks, are in reality — the smallest of them — three feet high; generally they come up to our chests. We go up at the left hand corner . . . the Arabs push and pull me; I am quickly exhausted, it is desperately tiring. . . . The sun was rising just opposite; the whole valley of the Nile, bathed in mist, seemed to be a still white sea; and the desert behind us, with its hillocks of sand, another ocean, deep purple, its waves all petrified." Today you can no longer climb the Giza pyramids — centuries of scrambling tourists have taken too great a toll. But when I was a child in the 1940s, the Great Pyramid was always covered with striving figures, most of them khaki-clad — members of the British, French, New Zealand, Australian, Canadian, and other armed forces engaged in the Libyan campaign. Those who got to the top must have seen very much

Head of Ramesses II, Ramesseum, Thebes, 1993

Four Colossi of the Great Temple of Ramesses II, Abu Simbel, 1993

the same scene as did Flaubert. Cairo was then a city of one million people — bigger indeed than in the mid-nineteenth century, but nothing like the megalopolis of fourteen million that it is today, with its outer suburbs lapping the pyramids and the Sphinx.

And for the frustrated pyramid climbers of today, photography serves as a substitute. The aerial view provided by Marilyn Bridges is not too far different from the one you would get from the summit of the Great Pyramid — without the dismaying experience of hauling yourself up chest-high blocks of stone.

Flaubert came to Egypt in pursuit of the mysterious orient, as did so many of his contemporaries. For the prosperous nineteenth-century traveler, the Nile Valley was as essential an objective as the European Grand Tour. Hired dahabeahs plied the river by the score. Thomas Cook, the travel agency, began life in Egypt with Cook's tours taking the less adventurous upriver in cruise boats. Most came and went during a season, but the more committed stayed for years — the Egyptologists and those like Lucie Duff Gordon, victims of the nineteenth century's scourge disease, tuberculosis, who came to that hot dry climate in search of a few more years of life. Those whose commentaries have outlived them become in a fascinating way themselves a part of the continuing resonances of the place. When I looked at the pyramids as a child, I saw simply a familiar shape — albeit a somewhat impressive one. Now, they conjure up a whole miscellany of thoughts — the facts and figures of their construction, the attached mythologies, and perhaps above all the associations with the whole sequence of those who have come briefly under their spell. Herodotus, meticulously recording the method of their construction. Napoleon, commissioning an exhaustive survey. Flaubert, gasping his way up the huge blocks. Merely a few of the more eloquent testimonies to the effect that the monuments have had upon those who passed by, century after century.

Who could not be affected by the revelations of that extraordinary place? For the Victorian visitor, there was the unsettling reflection that here was the record of an ancient civilization whose technical achievements and spiritual complexity cast a shadow over the intellectual and scientific exuberance of their own time. This evidence of past sophistication threw doubts on the idea of history as a system of continuous progress. The monuments of European prehistory were primitive by comparison with the constructions of the Nile Valley. A blow had been dealt to Eurocentrism. The tombs, the temples, all the evidence of that way of life and of the knowledge and abilities of those people made it clear that what we think of as civilization had its origins here and not in France or Italy or Germany or along the banks of the Thames.

A portentous past is a mixed blessing for a country. Tourism is one of Egypt's main industries today, and ever has been. The great archaeological sites of the Nile Valley have always taken center stage, eclipsing the present. They have been a source of revenue, but have also given the unthinking visitor the impression of a place in which everything has already happened, where what goes on now is nothing but an accessory to what went before. But to my mind, far more potent is the extraordinary sense of continuity bestowed by those great calm presences. It is not so much the miracle of their continued existence as the reminder of the tenacity of human lives. Innumerable generations have come and gone, but this landscape is still peopled with the descendants of those who hacked out the stone, who adorned the temples. More than that, even over these thousands of years there is still an eerie reflection of today in the scenes within the tombs, those vivid frescoes that depict life beside the Nile back then. The papyrus reeds, the lotus flowers. The skeins of flying ducks, the ibis and the egret. Admittedly the crocodiles are gone now, shot out in the last century, and the hippos and the small desert lions, but the people don't look that different, if you imagine them in the stiff kilts of Pharaonic dress instead of the flowing galabiah of today.

To make that journey up the Nile — even in a modern air-conditioned cruise boat — is to follow one of the oldest routes in the world. "Eau de Nil" — the river has even given its name to a color, though in fact the water of the Nile is a sort of dun color rather than soft green. But, that being said, it is as fickle as the rest of that landscape, according to the time of day and the effect of the strong clear desert light. In the middle of the day the whole place quivers with heat, the water is brown and dense, the desert is blinding white. But by evening the light drains away, the water becomes deep blue, the line of the hills a burning orange and the sky apricot, primrose, and at last velvety black with the sizzling stars surely far nearer than in our hazy northern skies. It is a landscape of soft colors — the fawn and buff of sand and rock, the blue-green of sugarcane fields and of the ubiquitous feathery palms whose swaying fronds give the whole place a sense of light movement. To pass through the midst of this is to realize how everything centers upon the river. The villages line its banks, traffic between them goes by water quite as much as by land — flat-bottomed barges collecting bricks or bales of sugarcane, or delivering a consignment of camels, while lighter cargoes are carried in the slim feluccas with their swooping single white sail. It is a scene of intricate and complex activity, played out against the unchanging background of the great artery of the river, its birds and plants, and above all the glimpses of a temple, a rock-cut tomb, or some mysterious unidentifiable edifice to remind you of the great depth of the past and the immutability of stone, sand, and water. The Colossi of Memnon preside over fields scratched from the rim of the desert, the Step Pyramid seems to be trying to melt away into the sand, the Abu Simbel figures stare enigmatically into the glittering sea of Lake Nasser.

The aerial journey undertaken by Marilyn Bridges and reflected in her photographs gives a fascinating extra dimension to that Nile voyage. We see the place quite differently, stripped of the human element, without the sounds and smells, and translated into a world of eloquent silence. Just as the desert light intensifies color, so her photography enhances the contrasts of light and shade, the depth of shadows, the clarity of detail. This splendid collection of photographs gives a privileged view of the Nile Valley. They set the monuments of antiquity within context — here presiding over the ancillary clutter of modern buildings, there stark against the sand and rock. They look both larger and smaller than they really are — larger when their vast shadows eclipse everything around, smaller when picked out as a distant sculptural shape against the curves of the river and the desert. Above all, they are arresting, emphatic, and deliberate presences amid the random features of natural landscape, their human derivation emphasized. Their permanence is subtly accentuated; they become alien presences in the contemporary world.

LOWER EGYPT

THREE PYRAMIDS OF GIZA, 1984

ABOVE: BURIAL PITS OF SOLAR BOATS, PYRAMID OF KHUFU, GIZA, 1993

OPPOSITE: PYRAMID OF KHEPHREN, GIZA, 1993

Pyramid of Menkaure, Giza, 1992

Pyramid of Khufu, Giza, 1992

Great Sphinx and Horses, Giza, 1984

GREAT SPHINX, GIZA, 1992

Overview of Abusir, 1992

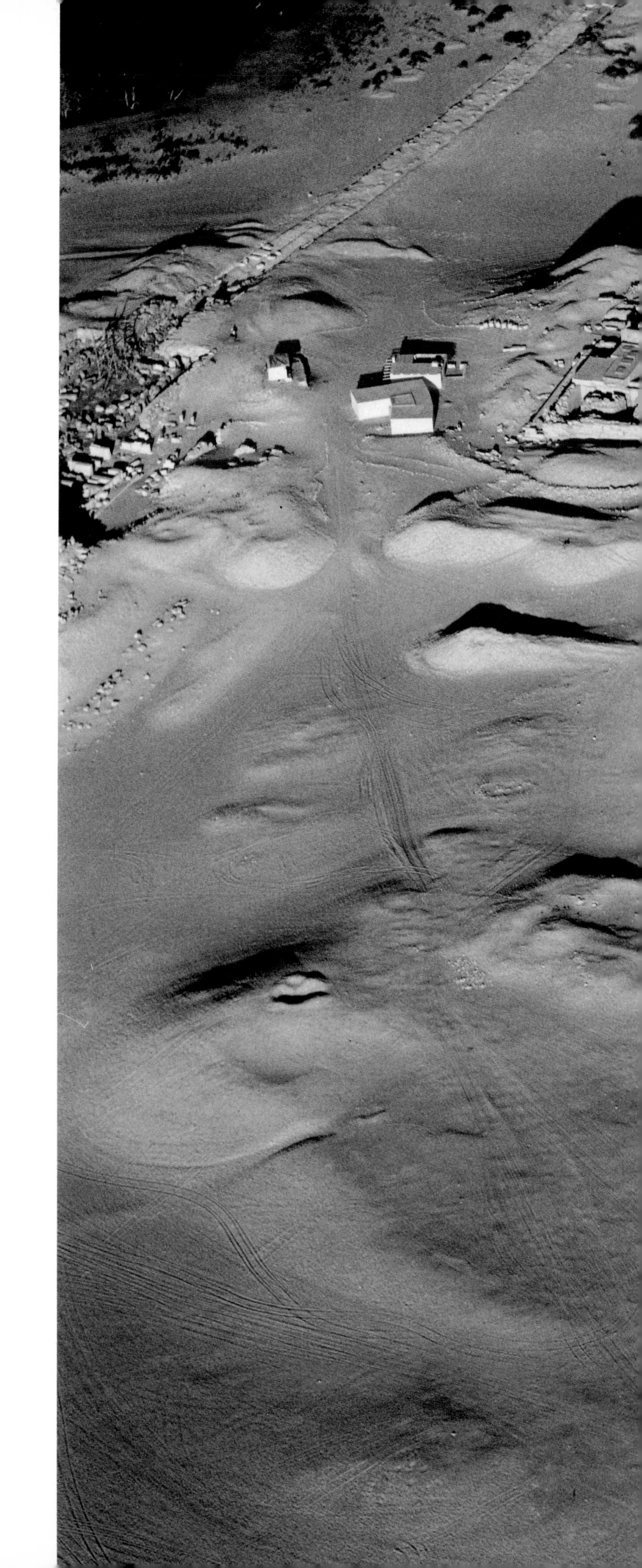

Pyramids of Neferirkare' and Neuserre' from Southwest, Abusir, 1993

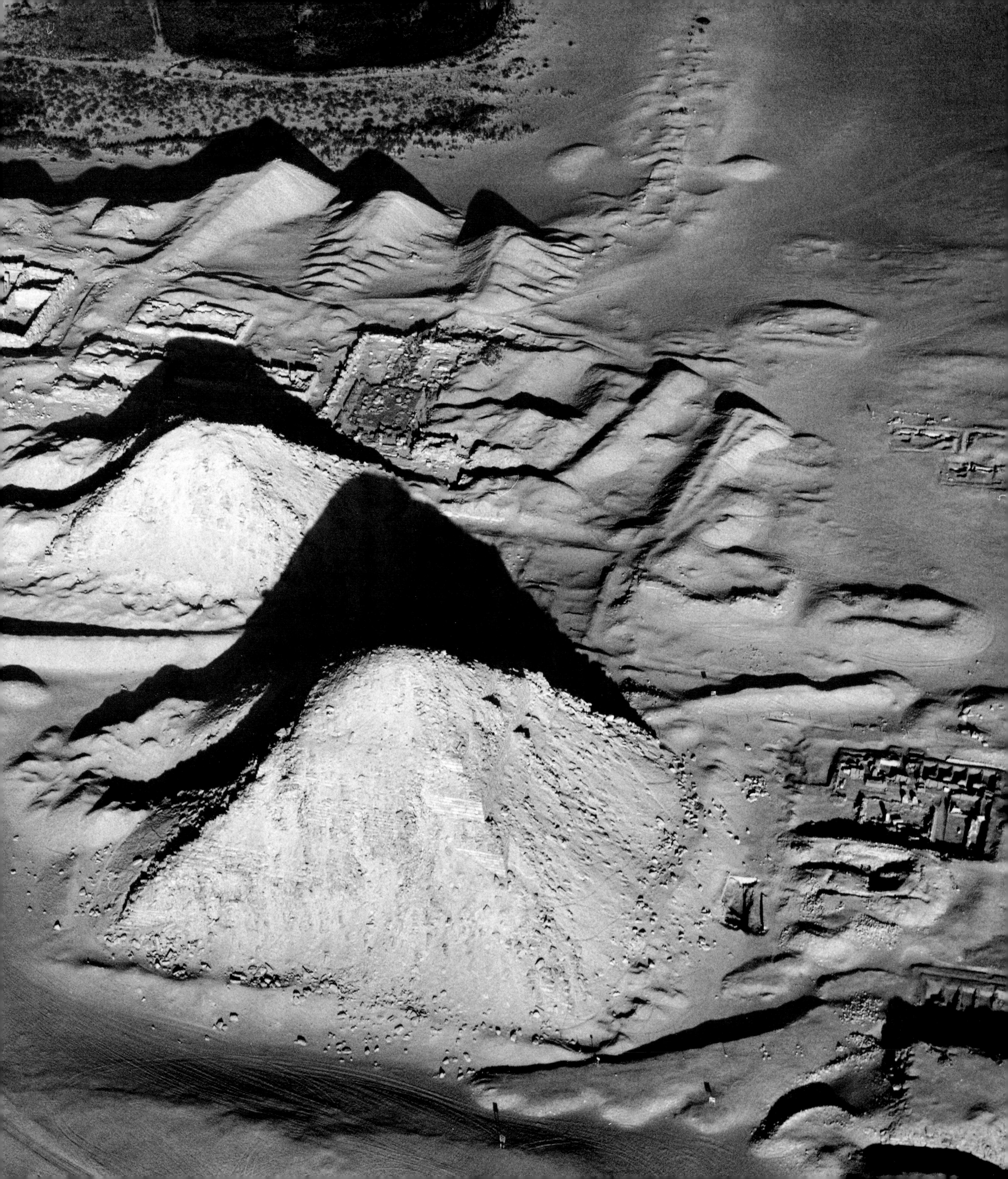

Mastaba of Ptahshepses, Abusir, 1992

SUN TEMPLE OF USERKAF, ABUSIR, 1993

ABOVE: STEPPED PYRAMID OF DJOSER, SAQQARA, 1992

OPPOSITE: STEPPED PYRAMID OF DJOSER WITH SHADOW, SAQQARA, 1993

The Pyramid of Pepy I from the Northeast, Saqqara, 1993

PYRAMID OF UNAS, SAQQARA, 1992

Bent Pyramid (Closeup), Dahshur, 1992

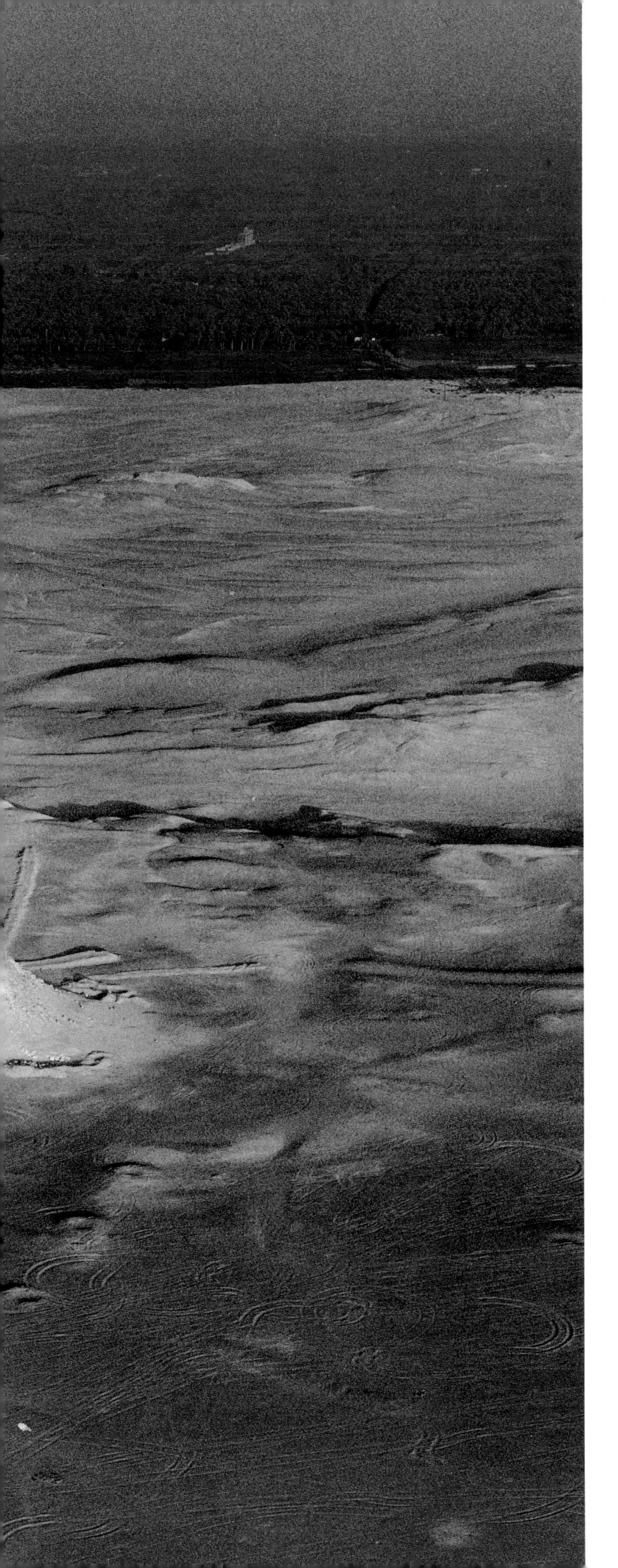

Bent Pyramid at Dahshur, 1992

Tomb of Haremhab, Saqqara, 1993

Tombs Along the causeway of Unas, Saqqara, 1993

Rock Formations, el-Faiyum, 1992

Pyramid of Amenemhet III (Southern Brick Pyramid), looking South, Dahshur, 1992

ABOVE: MASTABET EL-FARA'UN, SAQQARA, 1992

OPPOSITE: PYRAMID OF USERKAF, SAQQARA, 1992

Northern Stone Pyramid with Shadow, Dahshur, 1992

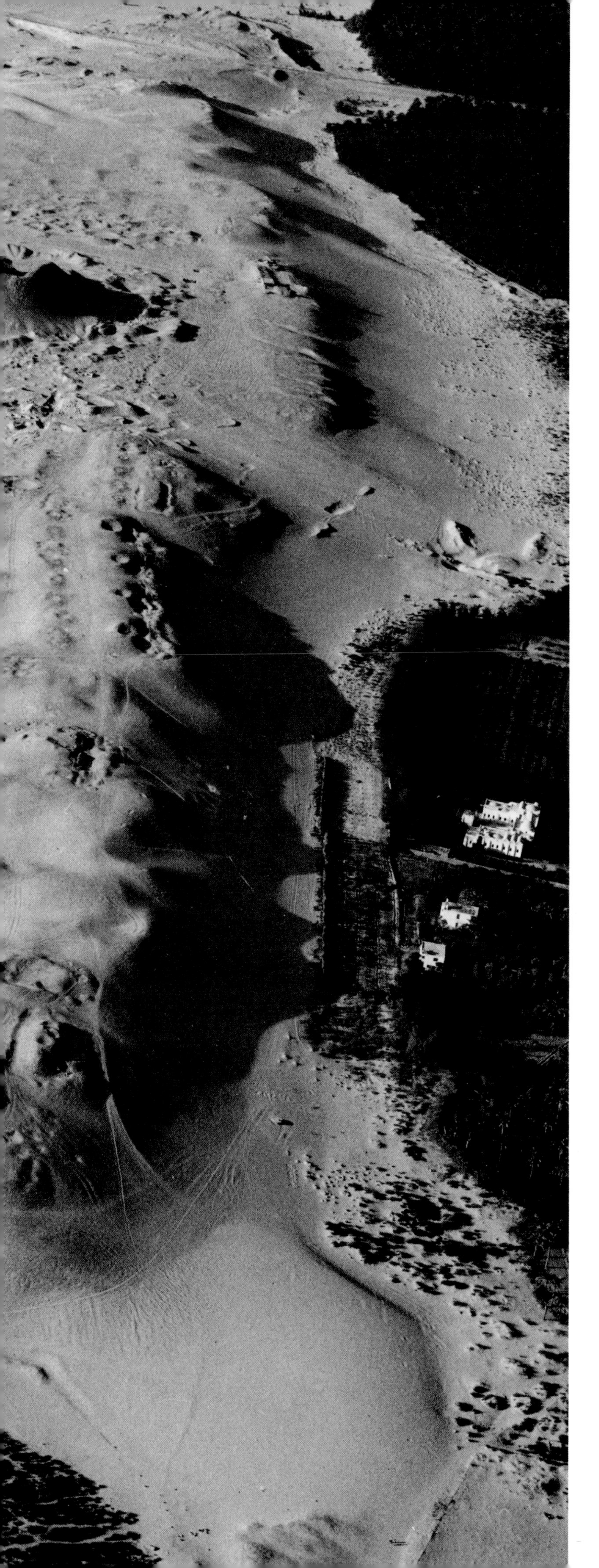

FACTORY AND PYRAMID OF SENWOSRET III, DAHSHUR, 1993

Pyramid of Amenemhet I, el-Lisht, 1992

Pyramid of Maidum, 1992

Islamic Tombs and Shrine, Medinet el-Faiyum, 1992

THEBES

Karnak with Sacred Lake (Overview from Northwest), 1993

Great Courtyard of Temple of Amun from the West, Karnak, 1993

Section of the Great Temple of Amun from the South, Karnak, 1993

ABOVE: ENTRANCE TO THE TEMPLE, LUXOR, 1992

OPPOSITE: TEMPLE OF LUXOR (OVERVIEW WITH CITY), 1993

MEDINET HABU, THEBES, 1993

Temple of Khons, Karnak, 1993

Colossi of Memnon, West Bank, Thebes, 1993

Deir el-Medina, West Bank, Thebes, 1993

TOMBS ON SHEIKH 'ABD EL-QURNA, WEST BANK, THEBES, 1993

Cemetery of Deir el-Medina, West Bank, Thebes, 1993

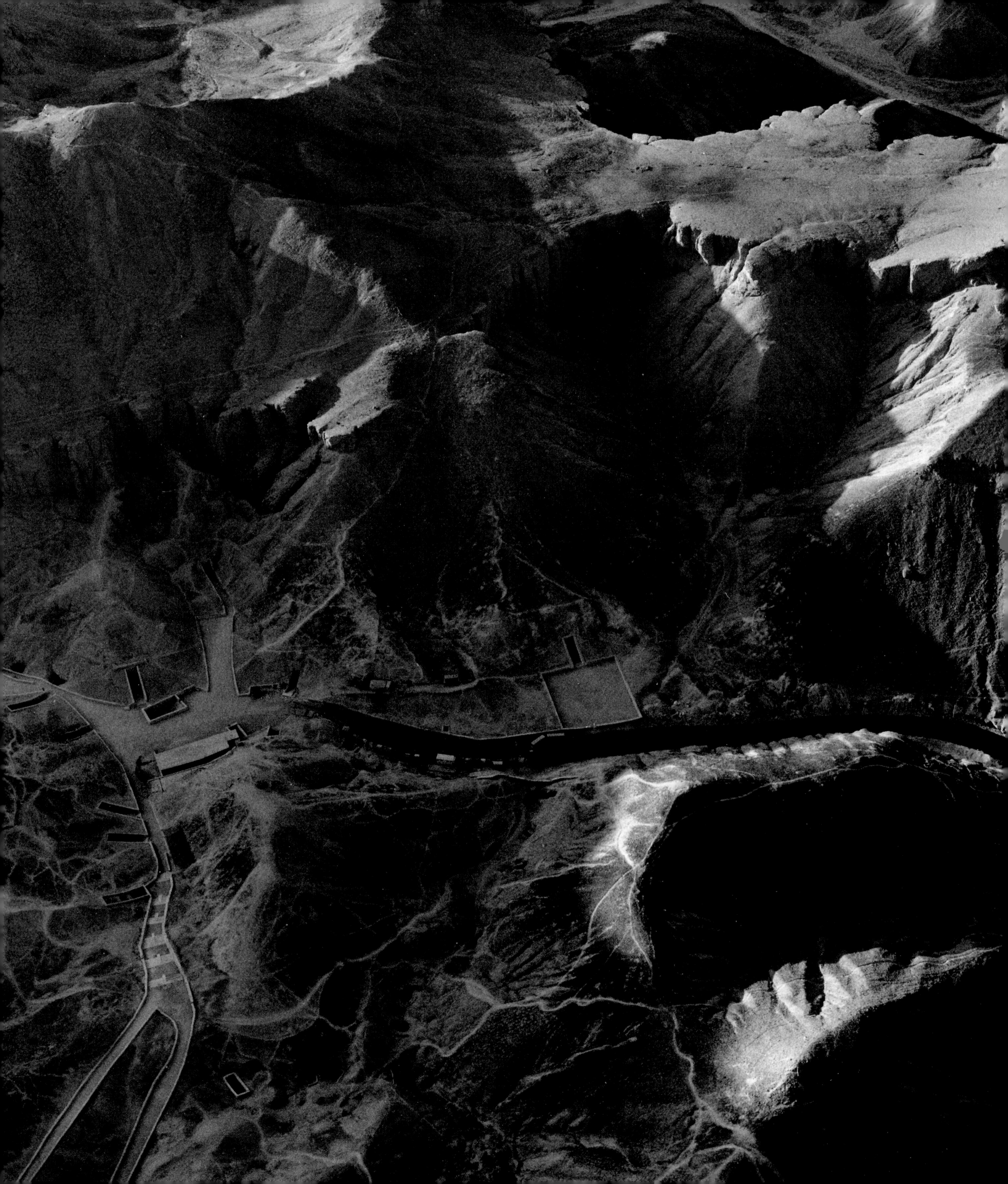

Valley of the Kings, West Bank, Thebes, 1993

Necropolis, Asasif Valley, West Bank, Thebes, 1993

Tomb of Ramose at Sheikh 'Abd el-Qurna, West Bank, Thebes, 1993

Coptic Monastery of Deir el-Mohareb, Thebes, 1993

The Temples at Deir el-Bahri, 1993

UPPER EGYPT

ROCK-CUT TOMBS OF BENI-HASAN, 1992

Temple of Hathor, Dendara, 1992

Islamic Tombs near Beni-Hasan, 1992

Temple of Khnum, Esna, 1992

Overview of Edfu, 1992

Temple of Horus at Edfu, 1992

PHILAE FROM THE EAST, 1992

TOMBS OF QUBBET EL-HAWA, ASWAN, 1992

Feluccas Along the Banks of the Nile, Aswan, 1992

MONASTERY OF ST. SIMEON, ASWAN, 1992

Temple of Sobek and Haroeris with River (Overview), Kom Ombo, 1992

MAUSOLEUM OF THE AGA KHAN, ASWAN, 1992

Great Temple of Ramesses II, Abu Simbel, 1993

Abu Simbel and Lake Nasser (Overview), 1993

Notes on the Photographs

Lower Egypt

Three Pyramids of Giza with Cairo, 1993 (page 10)

The sprawling suburbs of Cairo form a backdrop to the pyramids. Upper right is Nazlet el-Sammân, the village that sits on the valley temple of Khufu and on the pyramid city of the three kings. Upper left is the site of the village of Embaba, the battlefield for Napoleon's defeat of the Mamluks in 1798.

Three Pyramids of Giza, 1984 (page 19)

The three pyramids of Giza, built during the 4th Dynasty (2575–2465 B.C.) represent the apex of pyramid construction. In the foreground is the Pyramid of Khufu, who reigned 2551–2528 B.C. It stands 480 feet in height, and like all of the pyramids of Giza, it is oriented to the four cardinal directions, with its entrance on the north side. To its immediate right is the western mastaba field, with the remains of hundreds of freestanding, rectangular tombs of notables and functionaries. Next is the Pyramid of Khephren (2520–2494 B.C.), the second largest of the Giza pyramids at 470 feet. The third pyramid, rising 215 feet, is the smallest of the three and was built for Menkaure (2490–2472 B.C.). The small pyramid to its left is the tomb of one of Menkaure's queens. All of the pyramids have a core made of local limestone faced with fine limestone from the east bank, still preserved on the upper third of the Pyramid of Khephren. The lower portions of the casing of the Pyramid of Khephren and that of Menkaure consisted of red granite.

Pyramid of Khephren, Giza, 1993 (page 20)

Seen from the west, the shadow of the Pyramid of Khephren stretches across the vast necropolis. Immediately above (or east), and covered by the shadow, is its mortuary temple. A causeway leads from this temple across the central field of mastabas and rock-cut tombs, passing by the Great Sphinx (upper right-hand corner), seen here from the rear. Upper left is the south face of the Pyramid of Khufu. Above (east of) this pyramid are the smaller pyramids for Khufu's queens and daughter and a large cemetery for other relatives. On its right (south side) is a row of large mastabas belonging to high dignitaries and a boat pit covered by a modern, on-site boat museum.

Burial Pits of Solar Boats, Pyramid of Khufu, Giza, 1993 (page 21)

Three boat pits fall under the shadow of the east side of the Pyramid of Khufu. In the extreme right-hand corner of the photograph, a boat pit has been covered by a modern museum. In the 1950s a complete but detached wooden boat made of cedar was found here. It was 140 feet in length and had a displacement of almost 40 tons. Some of the boats may have been used at the funeral proceedings, while others were perhaps meant to provide the dead king with a means of transport in the afterlife. Also seen in this photograph are the three small pyramids built for Khufu's queens and a daughter and various mastabas of notables and family members.

Pyramid of Menkaure, Giza, 1992 (page 22)

Known as the "Divine Pyramid," this monument was built for Menkaure or Mycerinus (2490–2472 B.C.), and finished by his son and successor, Shepseskaf, the last king of the 4th Dynasty. The pyramid was refurnished some eighteen hundred years later during the 26th Dynasty, when the cult of the kings buried at Giza was revived. The two small step pyramids (below) are those of Menkaure's queens. The third small pyramid is considered to be the cult pyramid of the king. Facing the east side of the pyramid, and partly in shadow, are the remains of a mortuary temple.

Pyramid of Khufu, Giza, 1992 (page 23)

The Great Pyramid of Khufu (Cheops), built for the second king of the 4th Dynasty (2551–2528 B.C.), reaches 480 feet, making it the tallest of the Giza pyramids (its top courses have deteriorated and the cap-stone has disappeared). According to the Greek historian Herodotus, it took twenty years and one hundred thousand men to complete. The pyramid is surrounded by various mastabas and rock-cut tombs. To the left are small pyramids built for Khufu's queens and a daughter and two exposed boat pits. Upper left, abutting the central mastaba field, is the Great Sphinx, seen from the side, its rear facing a long causeway that stretches to the east wall of the Pyramid of Khephren (top right).

Great Sphinx and Horses, Giza, 1984 (pages 24–25)

Great Sphinx, Giza, 1992 (page 27)

The Great Sphinx, much weathered by time and sand, is undergoing restoration. Given its fragile nature, this monument's survival may be attributed to its burial under desert sands for much of its existence. Built during the 4th Dynasty (2575–2465 B.C.) out of rock left over from the quarrying operations of the Pyramid of Khephren, it is nearly 240 feet long and 65 feet high. Sphinxes are composite animals, with a lion's body and the head of a falcon, ram, or human. The Great Sphinx is a lion couchant with a human head, possibly representing King Khephren. On the head is the royal headdress. In the foreground, at the feet of the Sphinx, is the so-called Sphinx temple, which, apparently, was never finished. It differs from most buildings in the necropolis in that it does not serve a funerary function, and may have been dedicated to the sun god, Re'. To its immediate right is the partially restored, small temple of Amenophis II, which dates to the 18th Dynasty. Left of the Sphinx temple is the valley temple of Khephren, which is connected by a causeway (just left of the Sphinx) to the Pyramid of Khephren. Upper left is an area of numerous mastabas and rock-cut tombs. Behind the Sphinx, north of the causeway (upper center), can be seen the so-called Campbell's tomb, a huge tomb shaft of the 26th Dynasty.

Overview of Abusir, 1992 (pages 28-29)

The pyramids of Abusir date to the 5th Dynasty (2465–2323 B.C.). Although the founder of the dynasty, Userkaf, built his pyramid at Saqqara, four of the next five kings located their monuments at Abusir. Seen from the north (the entrance to each of the pyramids is the slightly depressed area on the north face), the pyramids (from front to back) are those of Sahure' (2458–2446 B.C.), Neuserre' (2416–2392 B.C.), Neferirkare' (2446–2426 B.C.), and the partially built pyramid of Ra'neferef (2419–2416 B.C.). The remains of mortuary complexes abut each pyramid on the east (left). The pyramid complex of Sahure' has suffered the least damage. Still visible to the left of its vast funerary structures is the outline of its causeway, which leads to the remains of a valley temple (raised slightly in the photograph). Also visible is the western portion of its enclosure wall. Lush cultivation borders the desert. The pyramids at Saqqara, some five miles distant, can be seen in a haze of sand and sun in the upper portion of the photograph.

Pyramids of Neferirkare' and Neuserre' from Southwest, Abusir, 1993 (pages 30–31)

The Pyramid of Neferirkare' (foreground) is the largest of the pyramids at Abusir and once rose to 230 feet (nevertheless, it was probably never quite finished). To the pyramid's right are associated mastabas of family members. The Pyramid of Neuserre' follows.

It was originally 170 feet in height. Its mortuary temple lies just above it in the photograph. Clearly visible is the mastaba of Ptahshepses (with its pillared court) toward the left-hand corner.

Mastaba of Ptahshepses, Abusir, 1992 (page 32)

The 5th Dynasty family mastaba of Ptahshepses (upper right), the vizier and son-in-law of Neuserre', is one of the largest mastaba tombs in Egypt, imitating the plan of a royal pyramid temple. The twenty square pillars of its large court are clearly visible. Upper left is the funerary complex of Neuserre', with its large mastabas for female members of the royal family and notables only partially exposed. The ridges in the foreground represent excavation debris from the 1902–1908 dig of the noted German archaeologist Ludwig Borchardt.

Sun Temple of Userkaf, Abusir, 1993 (page 33)

Found halfway between the pyramids of Abusir and Abu Gurab, the sun temple of Userkaf is the northernmost of Abusir's monuments. It was built during Userkaf's short reign of seven years (2465–2458 B.C.), and is the earliest preserved sun temple in Egypt. At the beginning of the 5th Dynasty, there was increased emphasis on the adoration of the sun god, and this temple is believed to be dedicated to Re'. Built partly of limestone and partly of Nile mud, it has dimensions of approximately 145 feet by 270 feet. An obelisk would have been a prominent feature of the temple complex. A causeway once linked the main temple to a small valley temple (upper left). The site was excavated by Swiss and German archaeologists in the mid 1950s.

Stepped Pyramid of Djoser, Saqqara, 1992 (page 34)

During the reign of Djoser or Netjerykhet (2630–2611 B.C.), second king of the 3rd Dynasty, the stepped pyramid evolved from the earlier mastaba tomb, an excavated substructure divided into a series of rooms and a central burial chamber on which a mud-brick superstructure was built. The pyramid rose in six unequal steps to a height of some 200 feet. Its base measurements were 460 feet by 388 feet. This is the earliest step pyramid built in Egypt and the forerunner of the familiar smooth-sided structure. Design has been attributed to Imuthes (Imhotep), celebrated as both physician and architect and finally deified as the god of medicine. Built to overlook the ancient city of Memphis, the pyramid was the central feature of a large complex of stone buildings and courtyards connected with the afterlife of the king. Around the perimeter of the complex was a massive stone enclosure (today covered by dunes, as at lower right). Seen here from the northwest, the mortuary temple of Djoser abuts the north side of the pyramid. The southeastern courtyard and various buildings on the east have been restored.

Stepped Pyramid of Djoser with Shadow, Saqqara, 1993 (page 35)

The shadow of the pyramid accentuates its irregular profile, while obscuring its east side and the so-called southern mansion and various auxiliary structures. Upper left is a court surrounded by chapels, which may have been erected on the occasion of the king's sed festival (or jubilee festivities), which in general commemorated the thirtieth year of a king's reign. In the court at the upper right is a B-shaped structure that is thought to be a marker used during the king's ceremonial run at the sed festival.

The Pyramid of Pepy I from the Northeast, Saqqara, 1993 (page 36)

The Pyramid of Pepy I (2289–2255 B.C.), second king of the 6th Dynasty, was nearly 175 feet in height and rose from a 258-foot-square base. It is located in the southern sector of Saqqara, where many pyramids have been robbed of their stone over the centuries for local building materials. Restoration of its associated temples, courtyards, and funerary buildings has been undertaken by a French mission since the 1950s. The 6th Dynasty was marked by the decline of the power of kings and the rise of independence of local principalities. Egypt may have lost control of Nubia during this period. To the left of the pyramid are the remains of three smaller queen's pyramids, now exposed and offering a view of their burial chambers.

Pyramid of Unas, Saqqara, 1992 (page 37)

Seen from the northwest, the Pyramid of Unas or Wenis (2356–2323 B.C.), last king of the 5th Dynasty, lies near the southwest corner of Djoser's pyramid enclosure and courtyard (extreme left). It once rose to a height of 142 feet from a square base of 190 feet, and was known in ancient times as "The Pyramid which is Beautiful of Places." The interior walls of the pyramid contain the earliest pyramid texts (funerary inscriptions). A small chapel faces its entrance on the north (left) side. East are the faint remains of its mortuary temple, which is linked to a ritual causeway, on both sides of which are mastabas and rock-cut tombs of the 5th and 6th Dynasties. Northeast of the pyramid is the double mastaba of Nebt and Khenut, Unas's wives. Two boat pits lie south of the causeway where it turns on a slight angle. Upper right is the 18th Dynasty Tomb of Haremhab.

Bent Pyramid (Closeup), Dahshur, 1992 (page 39)

Much of the original exterior casing of Snofru's pyramid remains intact. Abutting its south enclosure is the secondary pyramid (upper right).

Bent Pyramid at Dahshur, 1992 (pages 40–41)

Only 1.25 miles separate the pyramids of Dahshur from the Saqqara necropolis. It was at Dahshur that the radical move from the stepped pyramid to the true pyramid was completed at the beginning of the 4th Dynasty. The so-called Bent Pyramid (the earliest pyramid to be planned as a true pyramid from its start) gets its name from its unusual shape, probably the result of a last-minute correction to fix a structural fault in the then experimental design. Its original height was 345 feet. Built for Snofru (2575–2551 B.C.), the founder of the 4th Dynasty, its original name translates as "The Southern Shining Pyramid." Near the south wall of its still visible enclosure is the so-called Small Pyramid, believed to have been built as a secondary pyramid for the king. It once rose to some 105 feet. In the lower half of the west side (facing side) of the main pyramid, one can see the western entrance of the pyramid as a minuscule black square. In the background, at the edge of cultivation, is the much-eroded Pyramid of Amenemhet III.

Tomb of Haremhab, Saqqara, 1993 (page 42)

To the southwest of the Pyramid of Unas lies the Tomb of Haremhab, the great commander of Tut'ankhamun's army, and himself king at the end of the 18th Dynasty (1319–1307 B.C.). Haremhab built this tomb before his accession to the throne. He was actually buried in a tomb later constructed in the Valley of the Kings near Thebes. Although funerary adornments from the Saqqara tomb first appeared in the nineteenth century, its whereabouts remained a mystery to all but looters until it was unearthed by archaeologists in the 1970s. The entrance to the tomb leads to a colonnaded courtyard surrounded by walls. Some rooms functioned as chapels. Others contained statues of Haremhab and Anubis, the jackal-headed god. Colored wall reliefs depict Haremhab's career. The tomb is flanked at the north (above) by the two similar tombs of Princess Tia (sister of Ramesses II) and her husband Maya.

Tombs Along the Causeway of Unas, Saqqara, 1993 (page 43)

The partially restored causeway of the Pyramid of Unas frames the remains (upper left) of numerous tombs of the New Kingdom, dating from the late 18th Dynasty to the time of Ramesses II. They were excavated by the University of Cairo. Several 5th Dynasty tombs, including those of court functionaries and priests, lie on both sides of the causeway (lower center).

Rock Formations, el-Faiyum, 1992 (page 44)

These eroded sand and limestone formations are the remnants of the earliest coastline of the Mediterranean, and are rich in plant, fish, and even dinosaur fossils. The remains of Neolithic cultures have been found on the terraces.

Pyramid of Amenemhet III (Southern Brick Pyramid) Looking South, Dahshur, 1992 (page 45)

Built for Amenemhet III (1844–1797 B.C.), the sixth king of the 12th Dynasty, this monument is in a serious state of disrepair. The pyramid was constructed of brick faced with limestone and once reached a height of 268 feet. It was Amenemhet III who first irrigated and settled the Faiyum, the largest and most important of Egypt's oases, and it was in the Faiyum at Hawara that Amenemhet built another pyramid to be his final resting place. The 12th Dynasty (1991–1783 B.C.) was a period of much prosperity and cultural flowering in Egypt. The rectangular pit (lower left) is the tomb of the 13th Dynasty King Hor.

Pyramid of Userkaf, Saqqara, 1992 (page 46)

The practice of building pyramids, which was abandoned by Shepseskaf, was resumed by the kings of the 5th Dynasty, although they were not built to the standards of their predecessors. Composed of a core of small stones with a facing of limestone, this pyramid has not withstood weathering over time. Userkaf (2465–2458 B.C.), founder of the 5th Dynasty, built his pyramid 160 feet high. Surrounding the pyramid in various degrees of ruin are its mortuary chapel (in the pyramid shadow), and a large statue temple to the south, just behind the pyramid. Its entrance faces north (or front).

Mastabet el-Fara'un, Saqqara, 1992 (page 47)

Located in Saqqara's southern necropolis, which borders Dahshur, the Mastabet el-Fara'un, seen here from the north, is the burial complex of Shepseskaf (2472–2467 B.C.). This last king of the 4th Dynasty abandoned the pyramid form for his tomb, substituting instead a structure some 330 feet by 240 feet, which resembles a huge rectangular sarcophagus. It is made of massive local limestone blocks 24 to 30 inches thick and faced with Tura limestone. The tomb was thoroughly looted in ancient times. On the east side of the tomb (left) are the scant remains of its mortuary temple, the stone of which was used elsewhere for building blocks.

Northern Stone Pyramid with Shadow, Dahshur, 1992 (page 49)

A shadow represents the pure pyramidal shape of the Northern Stone Pyramid. Located a short distance north of the Bent Pyramid, it was the second pyramid at Dahshur built by Snofru. Its original height was 340 feet. Its pyramid temple has recently been excavated by the German Archaeological Institute, Cairo.

Factory and Pyramid of Senwosret III, Dahshur, 1993 (pages 50–51)

Modern industrial encroachment threatens the vast necropolis of Dahshur. Here, the perimeters of a natural gas factory bear an uncomfortable likeness to the faint remains of the enclosure walls of the Pyramid of Senwosret III (upper right). Known as the

"Northern Brick Pyramid," it was nearly 260 feet high, and its original enclosure measured 630 feet by 730 feet. It was built for Senwosret III (1878–1841 B.C.), fifth king of the 12th Dynasty, a great warrior-king who subdued the Nubians and invaded the Levant. Nearby are mastabas and tombs for members of the royal family. When first excavated by the French in the 1890s, six wooden boats were found buried near the pyramid. Currently, it is being excavated by the Metropolitan Museum of Art (New York).

Pyramid of Amenemhet I, el-Lisht, 1992 (page 52)

Amenemhet I (1991–1962 B.C.), founder of the 12th Dynasty, moved his capital from Thebes to Itjawy, the location of which is still unknown. Its necropolis, however, is believed to be the pyramid field seen here at el-Lisht, some nineteen miles south of Dahshur. During the last years of Amenemhet's reign, Egypt expanded its power south, under the military leadership of his son and successor Senwosret I. Apparently, Amenemhet was murdered while his son was away campaigning in Libya. The Pyramid of Amenemhet I (seen here from the west) originally rose to some 180 feet. When constructing the inner core of the pyramid, a large number of limestone blocks were appropriated from Old Kingdom tombs at Dahshur, Saqqara, and Giza. Entrance to the pyramid is on the north side (or left). The pyramid is surrounded by unexcavated mastabas belonging to the royal family and high state officials. Excavation debris of the Metropolitan Museum of Art (New York) expedition of 1906–1922 fans out in the foreground of the photograph.

Pyramid of Maidum, 1992 (page 53)

Despite its appearance as a tower-shaped structure surrounded by stone rubble, this is the remains of the first true pyramid ever attempted in Egypt. Perhaps started under Huni (2599–2575 B.C.), the last king of the 3rd Dynasty, and probably finished by his successor, Snofru, it began as an eight-stepped structure, and then was redesigned with its sides filled in to form a proper pyramidal shape. Most of this later masonry of the true pyramid was eventually quarried away by stone robbers, exposing its original steps. A section of the casing of the true pyramid is visible at the lower left-hand corner. The view in the photograph is from the west. On the east the remains of a causeway can be seen. Just northeast of the pyramid is the 4th Dynasty mastaba of an unknown prince.

Islamic Tombs and Shrine, Medinet el-Faiyum, 1992 (pages 54–55)

Medinet el-Faiyum is the provincial capital of the Faiyum, an especially fertile region, often called an oasis, located about sixty miles southwest of Cairo. Much of the area was periodically under water in ancient times. Drainage and cultivation began in the historic period, with large-scale reclamation attempted in the 12th Dynasty.

THEBES

Karnak with Sacred Lake (Overview from Northwest), 1993 (pages 58–59)

The great temple complex of Karnak was the ancient Egyptian Ipet-isut, the center of Theban worship in Upper Egypt, which came into prominence at the beginning of the Middle Kingdom (2040–1640 B.C.), and for nearly two thousand years, its temples were built, enlarged, pulled down, added to, and restored. From the west, entrance to the complex is through the enormous Pylon I, which dates to the 30th Dynasty or the early Ptolemaic Period, and leads to the Temple of Amun, nominal head of the so-called Theban triad (which includes the companion gods Mut and Khons). The pylon is 370 feet wide and stands 143 feet high. Its walls are 49 feet thick. The Great Court follows, flanked north (left) and south with colonnades. The southern colonnade is interrupted by the entrance to the Temple of Ramesses III. In the middle of the courtyard are the remains of a kiosk of King Taharqa, with one of its columns standing. Pylon II (badly damaged) was built by Haremhab, and three statues of Ramesses II are found on each side of the entrance. Beyond this pylon are the Great Hypostyle Hall and other buildings of the temple proper. In the upper portion of the photograph is the sacred lake; a large granite scarab at its edge dates to the reign of Amenophis III (1391–1353 B.C.). Just to the right of the sacred lake and south of the temple proper are a series of collapsed pylons from the 18th Dynasty. They mark the southern access to the temple.

Great Courtyard of Temple of Amun from the West, Karnak, 1993 (pages 60–61)

Center of the courtyard are the remains of the kiosk of Taharqa (25th Dynasty). Statues of Ramesses II mark the entrance to the much-dilapidated second pylon. The Great Hypostyle Hall with its raised central alley of columns follows. In the foreground the west wall of Pylon I edges the small Temple of Ramesses III. In the upper portion of the photograph, outside the main temple enclosure, is the precinct of Montu, with the scant remains of a temple built by Amenophis III (1391–1353 B.C.) and dedicated to the war god and old local god of Thebes. Most prominent is the high gate of Ptolemy II and Ptolemy III (285–221 B.C.).

Section of the Great Temple of Amun from the South, Karnak, 1993 (page 63)

This central portion of the great temple is highlighted by the obelisks of Queen Hatshepsut (right) and Tuthmosis I, 18th Dynasty monarchs, standing in front of the remains of the fourth and fifth pylons. (The second obelisk erected by Hatshepsut and others has long since collapsed.) The two surviving obelisks are 97 feet and 71 feet in height. Upper left is the impressive hypostyle hall. Its roof (now gone) was supported by 134 papyrus columns. Relief decoration in the hall was completed during the reigns of Sethos I (1306–1290 B.C.) and Ramesses II (1290–1224 B.C.). Lower right are the remains of shrines and chapels in various states of preservation. At the lower right corner, we see the roof of the central bark shrine of Amun, decorated under Philip Arrhidaeus (323–316 B.C.).

Temple of Luxor (Overview with City), 1993 (page 64)

The temple lies on the south end of the modern city, some 1.5 miles south of Karnak, on the edge of the east bank of the Nile. Essentially built by two kings, Amenophis III, 1391–1353 B.C. (the inner part) and Ramesses II, 1290–1224 B.C. (the outer), with the great colonnade by Tut'ankhamun and minor additions made by Haremhab and Alexander the Great, the temple was dedicated to Amun, Mut, Khons, and the deified ruler. It is 623 feet long and 180 feet wide at its widest point, and is comprised of chapels dedicated to these deities, with their vestibules and subsidiary chambers, a large hypostyle hall, and an open peristyle court, approached from the north by a great colonnade. The temple was closely connected with the Great Temple of Amun at Karnak, and once a year, during the second and third months of the inundation season, a long religious festival was held at Luxor during which the image of Amun of Karnak visited his southern retreat.

Entrance to the Temple, Luxor, 1992 (page 65)

In the foreground is a modern plaza before the pylon of Ramesses II, which comprises the entrance to the temple. Two statues of Ramesses II, reaching 46 feet in height, are seated before the entrance, and the remains of four standing statues of the king are at their side. The obelisk (left of the entrance) is one of two originally on site. The other (its base still visible) has stood since 1836 in the Place de la Concorde in Paris. Beyond the pylon is the Court of Ramesses II, with seventy-four columns and the walls inscribed with scenes of the Min (fertility god) festival and other rituals. During the Ayyubid Period (thirteenth century A.D.), the little Mosque of Abu el-Haggag (left) was built in the courtyard. The entrance to the Processional Colonnade of Tut'ankhamun (with seven columns almost 52 feet high on either side) is flanked at the front by two seated colossi of Ramesses II with Queen Nefertari by his right leg and, behind the gate, by two seated double statues of Amun and Mut. The peristyle forecourt of Amenophis III follows. It is linked to the remainder of the temple, which is comprised of a hypostyle hall and various shrines and chapels.

Medinet Habu, Thebes, 1993 (page 66)

The ancient city of Thebes, which for nearly one thousand years (roughly 1991–1070 B.C.) formed the famed capital and religious center of Egypt, spread out over the area of present-day Luxor and Karnak, and extended its boundaries, with its vast necropolises and great royal mortuary temples, onto the west bank of the Nile and into the desert valleys to the west. The Medinet Habu temple complex (its name derived from a now abandoned Christian village) contained one of the earliest ritual centers in the Theban area to be associated closely with Amun. Highlight of the complex is the mortuary temple of Ramesses III, surrounded by a fortress-like enclosure wall, which has largely disappeared (remnants can be seen in front and upper left). The East Fortified Gate (upper right) leads to the main temple. Behind the gate is the original small temple of Amun (18th Dynasty). Below it and to the right are the mortuary chapels of the divine consorts, princesses who became the ecclesiastical rulers of Thebes in the late 25th and early 26 Dynasties. Below the pylon of Ramesses III are the remains of a royal palace used by the king during religious festivals.

Temple of Ramesses III, Medinet Habu, Thebes, 1993 (page 67)

The central portion of the great Temple of Ramesses III (1194–1163 B.C.) is well preserved. On the facade of the first pylon, with its four niches for flagpoles, are reliefs celebrating the king's military successes in the presence of Amun. Beyond the first pylon are a colonnaded courtyard, a second pylon, another court, the great hypostyle hall, and several cult temples, including the central bark shrine of Amun.

The Ramesseum from the South, West Bank, Thebes, 1993 (pages 68–69)

Lower right is the entrance to the Second Court, which was surrounded by colonnades and colossal statue pillars of the king. At the rear of the court, stairs lead to a raised terrace, part of the portico of which has four surviving statue pillars. A solitary adorned head from a collapsed colossus of Ramesses II rests on the ground before the portico. Beyond this point is the Great Hypostyle Hall, which like the hypostyle hall at Karnak, is divided into three higher central aisles and six lower lateral aisles. A portion of the roof is intact. The interior rooms with the main sanctuaries have long since been quarried away.

The Ramesseum (Overview), West Bank, Thebes, 1993 (page 70)

The mortuary complex of Ramesses II (seen here from the west) was dedicated to Amun and the cult of this renowned king, and consists of a main temple and surrounding brick-built storerooms and other buildings — all within an enclosure wall. Only about half of the original structure survives. A temple palace once stood to the right of the main structure. Ramesses II's tomb is in the Valley of the Kings. His rule of sixty-six years (1290–1224 B.C.) was a period of intense building activity. It has been estimated that nearly half of the surviving temples date from this time.

Temple of Khons, Karnak, 1993 (page 71)

At the southwest corner of Karnak's walled temple precinct, a gateway (lower right), known as the Bab el-'Amara and built by Ptolemy III Euergetes I (246–221 B.C.), leads to what was once a short avenue of sphinxes (later covered by a kiosk of four-by-five columns), which precedes the entrance to the Temple of Khons. Dedicated to the Theban moon god and son of Amun and Mut, the temple was built by Ramesses III (1194–1163 B.C.), but most of its reliefs were executed during the reigns of Ramesses IV (1163–1156 B.C.) and Ramesses XI (1100–1070 B.C.). The facility is entered by a large pylon, 105 feet long and 59 feet high, and consists of a colonnaded forecourt, a hypostyle hall, and several chapels. The walls of the temple are replete with reliefs. Adjoining the southwest side of the Temple of Khons is the small Temple of Opet (the hippopotamus goddess of childbirth and mother of Osiris) built by Ptolemy VIII Euergetes II (170–163, 145–116 B.C.). The structure leaning against the Khons temple (upper left) is a modern warehouse holding antiquities.

Colossi of Memnon, West Bank, Thebes, 1993 (pages 72–73)

These regal colossi stood guard at the entrance to a huge mortuary temple of Amenophis III (1391–1353 B.C.) long reduced to a faint trace behind the statues. The statues were carved from hard yellow-brown quartzite and represent the king seated on a throne. They reach 64 feet in height and are 20 feet across the shoulders. The weight of one statue alone (without its base) is estimated to be 800 tons.

Deir el-Medina, West Bank, Thebes, 1993 (page 75)

The New Kingdom workmen's village at Deir el-Medina is the remains of a walled settlement with some seventy houses, in which workmen (or rather artisans) who labored at the tombs in the Valley of the Kings lived with their families. More to the right is the little Temple of Dier el-Medina, which itself is surrounded by a high wall of sun-dried brick. The temple was begun in the reign of Ptolemy IV Philopator (221–205 B.C.) and completed under his successors. It was dedicated to the goddess Hathor. To the left of the village under a blanket of shadow are the tombs of the workmen themselves.

Tombs on Sheikh 'Abd el-Qurna, West Bank, Thebes, 1993 (page 76)

On the hill of Sheikh 'Abd el-Qurna, south of Deir el-Bahri, lies a large pillared tomb of the Middle Kingdom (2040–1640 B.C.) and other tombs of the New Kingdom (1540–1070 B.C.). In the background under shadow are the Temple of Hatshepsut (upper right) and the small valley where the royal mummies were found.

Cemetery of Deir el-Medina, West Bank, Thebes, 1993 (page 77)

These rock-cut tombs near the workmen's village at Deir el-Medina belong to the artisans and officials of the Theban necropolis. They date mostly to the 19th and 20th Dynasties, although a few tombs from the 18th Dynasty are also found here. Most of the tombs were marked by a small brick pyramid such as the one reconstructed in the center of the photograph. Above the tombs is the French expedition house.

Valley of the Kings, West Bank, Thebes, 1993 (pages 78–79)

The great necropolis known as the Valley of the Kings lies to the west of ancient Thebes and covers a desolate area of rocky escarpments and sand. Here vast tombs for the kings of the 18th to 20th Dynasties were cut out of rock, with passages and chambers intended for the interment of a sarcophagus and grave goods. Walls were inscribed with scenes depicting phases of the deceased's journey through the Underworld and his restoration to eternal life. The path (left in the foreground) passes by several 19th Dynasty tombs, including those of Sethos I and Ramesses I, before reaching an open way, just to the right of which is a modern rest house. Above this convenience, a little rectangle represents the entrance to the Tomb of Tut'ankhamun (1333–1323 B.C.), opened by Howard Carter and Lord Carnarvon in 1922, and yielding one of the largest and most valuable finds of grave goods ever made in Egypt. Just above Tut's tomb is the Tomb of Ramesses VI (1151–1143 B.C.). Continuing to the right and up an embankment is the Tomb of Merneptah (1224–1214 B.C.), the son and successor of Ramesses II. The celebrated monarch's tomb follows. Further right, with the facing courtyard, is the Tomb of Ramesses IV (1163–1156 B.C.). Except for Tut's tomb, all these tombs were rifled in antiquity, and as a precaution, many of the mummies were removed to a cache near Deir el-Bahri.

Necropolis, Asasif Valley, West Bank, Thebes, 1993 (pages 80–81)

The Asasif Valley, just east of Deir el-Bahri and the Temple of Hatshepsut (visible in upper left-hand corner), is the setting for a large Middle Kingdom to Late Period necropolis, the tombs of which are cut into the surrounding cliffs and cover the valley bottom. Two pylons lead from the modern road down into immersed tomb courts. The first (larger) leads to the mortuary complex of Montemhet, a Theban prince of the 25th and 26th Dynasties, who was an accomplished ruler of much of Upper Egypt during his lifetime. The second pylon marks the entrance to the Tomb of Pabasa, steward of Princess Nitocris, daughter of Psammetichus I (664–610 B.C.), second king of the 26th Dynasty. At the extreme left (middle) is the pillared facade of the tomb of Djari, a courtier of King Mentuhotpe II (2061–2010 B.C.). In the foreground is the former excavation house of the Metropolitan Museum of Art.

Tomb of Ramose at Sheikh 'Abd el-Qurna, West Bank, Thebes, 1993 (page 83)

Located in the rocky hills between Deir el-Bahri and the Ramesseum, the rock tombs of Sheikh 'Abd el-Qurna represent the most important group of private tombs built for dignitaries and priests during the New Kingdom (1550–1070 B.C.). Center is the Tomb of Ramose, set among the houses of the present-day inhabitants of western Thebes. Ramose was governor of Thebes and vizier under Amenophis IV (1353–1335 B.C.). The tomb was left unfinished when the capital was moved from Thebes to Tell el-Amarna in the north.

Coptic Monastery of Deir el-Mohareb, Thebes, 1993 (page 84)

A necropolis surrounds the modern structure with its dome-shaped tombs. The shape of the tombs follows an ancient tradition that goes back to the Roman Period.

The Temples at Deir el-Bahri, 1993 (page 85)

The mortuary temples of Deir el-Bahri, built at the foot of sheer desert cliffs by Nebhepetre' Mentuhotpe, 2061–2010 B.C. (left), and Queen Hatshepsut, 1473–1458 B.C. (right), were dedicated to the joint cult of Amun and the ruler. A sanctuary for Hathor, the necropolis goddess of Thebes, was added to the left side of the Temple of Hatshepsut. Shortly after the completion of Hatshepsut's temple, Tuthmosis III (1479–1425 B.C.) built a temple complex for the god Amun above the two and a chapel for Hathor between the two temples. The Temple of Mentuhotpe (enveloped in shadow) was the first temple in Egypt built on a terrace ascended by a ramp. The Temple of Hatshepsut, some 550 years younger, is a partly rock-cut but mostly freestanding terraced structure. Two ramps lead from the Lower Court to the final Upper Court, with its sanctuary, and past various colonnades and the remains of chapels and shrines. In the foreground is a rectangular opening known as Bab el-Hosan, a long underground passage leading to a statue burial connected to the Temple of Mentuhotpe.

UPPER EGYPT

Rock-Cut Tombs of Beni Hasan, 1992 (page 88)

These tombs, thirty-nine in all, were constructed during the Middle Kingdom (2040–1640 B.C.), and formed the most important provincial necropolis on the east bank of the Nile between Memphis and Asyut. Several of the tombs belong to the "Great Overlords of the Oryx (or Antelope) nome," the 16th nome (or province) of Upper Egypt. The tombs are lined with inscriptions and vivid representations of everyday life in the provinces. Here, we see the southern group (tombs nos. 14–26), including tomb no. 17 of the nomarch Khety (behind the two guards).

Temple of Hathor, Dendara, 1992 (page 89)

Ancient Dendara was the capital of the 6th nome of Upper Egypt and a principal center for the cult of Hathor, the bovine goddess of love and joy. Its temple complex, situated on the west bank, is oriented, as was customary, toward the Nile, and measures nearly 315 yards by 305 yards. It is enclosed by a wall of bricks, at points 40 feet thick and rising to a height of about 33 feet, and was entered by a monumental gateway that dates from the time of Domitian and Trajan (Roman emperors of the first century A.D.). Inside (and to the right) are the remains of several buildings. In the foreground is the so-called birth house from the time of Trajan. Behind is a Coptic church, which dates to the late fifth century A.D., and a Roman sanatorium. The dominant monument in the complex is the wonderfully preserved Temple of Hathor, built between the first century B.C. and the first century A.D., although it was never quite finished. Its forecourt leads to a colonnaded vestibule *(pronaos),* a large hypostyle hall, and various antechambers and sanctuaries. The square to the right of the temple, once a sacred lake, is now an arboreal basin. In the desert behind is a large Pharaonic cemetery.

Islamic Tombs near Beni Hasan, 1992 (pages 90–91)

Temple of Khnum, Esna, 1992 (page 92)

The remains of the Temple of Khnum are surrounded by the sprawling urbanity of Esna, a small country town on the left bank of the Nile, thirty-four miles south of Luxor. The city, known in antiquity as Tasenet (Latopolis to the Greeks), was once an important district center in Upper Egypt. Its Temple of Khnum, of which only its well-preserved *pronaos* remains, dates to the first century A.D. It was dedicated to Khnum, the ram-headed local god, and his associate goddesses Neith and Heka. The facade, which features six columns, faces east. It is 121 feet long and 49 feet high. The roof of the *pronaos* is supported by 24 columns.

Overview of Edfu, 1992 (page 93)

Edfu seen from the northeast rises above the wide valley around it. In ancient times it was the capital of the 2nd nome of Upper Egypt. Parts of the ancient city are under the modern town, and excavations have revealed other remains on the mound above its Temple of Horus, the most completely preserved temple in Egypt. Dedicated to the hawk-headed god Horus, son of Osiris and Isis, the temple was initiated in 237 B.C. under Ptolemy III Euergetes I and finished in 57 B.C.

Temple of Horus at Edfu, 1992 (pages 94–95)

For unknown reasons the Temple of Horus at Edfu is oriented to the south instead of the north. The temple is the main structure of a much larger complex surrounded by enclosure walls, part of which can be seen. A birth house from the Ptolemaic Period abuts its entrance. Large dramatic reliefs highlight the temple's pylons. Beyond lies a colonnaded forecourt and the temple proper, with a covered hypostyle hall, several antechambers with shrines and altars, and finally a large sanctuary. To the left (west) of the complex are remains of the ancient city.

Philae from the East, 1992 (pages 96–97)

Between 1972 and 1980, an international rescue operation saved the temples of Philae from the rising waters of Lake Nasser (which eventually submerged the island) and deposited them on the small island of Agilkia to the northwest, which is pictured here. Most of the buildings were erected in the last two centuries B.C. and the first century A.D. The layout of ancient Philae on Agilkia is not complete. Several structures remain on the sunken Philae with the intent to recover them at a later date. The Temple of Isis (center), oriented from north to south, with its extraordinary double pylons, was the architectural climax of Philae. The temple was entered from the south (left), first by going through its outer court, flanked by colonnades. After passing through the forecourt between the first and second pylons, one enters the temple proper, which consists of a vestibule, several antechambers, a sanctuary, and subsidiary chapels. The colonnaded structure below the temple is a kiosk of the Roman Period.

Tombs of Qubbet el-Hawa, Aswan, 1992 (page 99)

Located on the west bank, across the Nile from Aswan, Qubbet el-Hawa, the "Dome of the Wind," contains rock-cut tombs of Old Kingdom (2575–2134 B.C.) officials and Middle Kingdom (2040–1640 B.C.) nomarchs. In the foreground is the Tomb of Prince Sarenput I, who lived during the reign of Senwosret I (1971–1926 B.C.). Crowning the hill is a small sheikh's tomb, to the left of which (in the photograph) is Kitchener's Island, once owned by Lord Kitchener, and now a botanical garden. At the extreme upper left is the Hotel Aswan Oberoi on the island of Elephantine.

Feluccas Along the Banks of the Nile, Aswan, 1992 (pages 100–101)

Feluccas are triangular-sail vessels that date to ancient times and were the traditional vehicle of commerce along the Nile, the lifeblood of Egyptian civilization. Ancient Egypt's sails were not confined to river commerce. In fact, the seafaring exploits of her navy were legendary. Egypt's boats sailed the Mediterranean as far as the Black Sea and Gibraltar, and in the Red Sea, they passed through the Gulf of Oman and into the Indian Ocean in search of discoveries and trading partners. These feluccas are on the west bank slightly down river from the Villa Nur el-Salam (center right).

Monastery of St. Simeon, Aswan, 1992 (page 102)

On a hill opposite Aswan on the west bank of the Nile are the ruins of the Monastery of St. Simeon (Simon), founded in the seventh century A.D. and abandoned in the thirteenth because of a dwindling water supply. Its walls of undressed stone and sun-dried brick are almost 20 feet tall.

Temple of Sobek and Haroeris with River (Overview), Kom Ombo, 1992 (page 103)

Located 25 miles north of Aswan on an elevated bend of the Nile, ancient Kom Ombo was an important administrative and commercial center during the Ptolemaic Period (304–30 B.C.). Its Temple of Sobek and Haroeris (seen here from the northwest) was started by Ptolemy VI Philometor (180–145 B.C.) and Ptolemy XII Auletes (80–51 B.C.) and completed in the Roman Period. Dedicated to two principal deities, the crocodile-headed god Sobek and the falcon-headed god Haroeris, each with its own rites and festivals, the temple was divided by an imaginary line along its longitudinal axis into two halves, each of which had its own gateways and doors, and its own chapel. Only the lower halves of sixteen columns that surrounded the forecourt still exist. The temple proper consists of a *pronaos* with fifteen columns, a hypostyle hall with ten support columns, three antechambers, and several chapels. Within the temple enclosure are (lower right) the remains of a birth house dating from the second century B.C., and (upper right) the Gate of Ptolemy XII Auletes. The small first-century A.D. Temple of Hathor, just next to it, is now used to store the mummies of sacred crocodiles from a nearby necropolis. A sacred well is found in the foreground of the precinct enclosure.

Mausoleum of the Aga Khan, Aswan, 1992 (pages 104–105)

The Mausoleum of the Aga Khan (Aga Khan III, Sultan Mohammed Shah, 1887–1957), the Iman spiritual head of the Knojas, a branch of the Ismaili sect, is situated on a hill on the west bank of the Nile opposite Aswan. According to the instructions of his widow, the former beauty queen Yvette Labrousse, whose Villa Nur el-Salam is in the foreground, a red rose is laid daily on the sarcophagus of the khan.

Great Temple of Ramesses II, Abu Simbel, 1993 (page 107)

The stupendous rock-cut facade of the Great Temple reaches some 100 feet in height and displays four colossal seated figures of Ramesses II, each nearly 70 feet tall (the second figure on the left lost its head and shoulders in ancient times). The four colossi represent the monarch in four deified modes. The king wears a head cloth and a double crown. He is adorned with a formal beard. In front of the colossi are much smaller (yet, still larger than life-size) figures of members of the royal family. The doorway behind the figures provides entrance to a large hypostyle hall, decorated with numerous representations of the king and his family. Beyond the hall is a vestibule and a sanctuary. Every year on February 20 and October 20, the rays of the rising sun penetrate into the sanctuary and fall upon the rear wall, illuminating the statues of the most important state gods of the period, Amun, Horus, and Ptah, and the figure of Ramesses II, an equal among gods.

Abu Simbel and Lake Nasser (Overview), 1993 (pages 108–109)

Between 1964 and 1968, the monumental rock temples at Abu Simbel on the west bank of the Nile were moved farther away from the river and to greater height in order to prevent them from being submerged under the rising waters of Lake Nasser. Left is the Great Temple of Ramesses II and to the right the Temple of Queen Nofretari. Both temples were built during the reign of Ramesses II (1290–1224 B.C.) to mark the thirtieth anniversary of his accession. Their original location, now under water, was just offshore in the area seen in the right foreground of the photograph.

MARILYN BRIDGES AND THE GODDESS SEKHMET

AFTERWORD

MARILYN BRIDGES

My first trip to Egypt in 1984 was brief. I had just completed a photographic project in Greece and decided spontaneously to tag on a three-day scouting trip to Egypt. I had always dreamed of walking among the pyramids of Giza and feeling their magical powers. I have long felt that these monuments were built on strong energy pathways that traverse the earth, and were intended to receive and transmit celestial energy. It is in my nature to find myself spiritually and discover my real self by entering new territory and leaving what is familiar behind. Most of my adult life has been spent exploring ancient sites such as the lines of Nazca in Peru, the standing stones of Great Britain, and Native American earthworks, and I have come to believe that ancient man was in touch with powers that we have long forgotten. Perhaps this is why I'm so attracted to photographing sacred sites. I want to stir these long-dormant feelings in others.

Not surprisingly, my experience of walking among the ruins inspired me to fly above them. After so many years of taking aerial photographs, the desire to visualize objects in the lap of the landscape is second nature. I soon realized, after making inquiries at the Cairo airport, that private aviation in Egypt is almost nonexistent. My attempt to locate a small, single-engine aircraft seemed hopeless. Frustrated, but still determined, I decided to go to the official flight training school of the Egyptian Air Force to find a way to get up into the air. I managed to charm my way in with a plea for help that the general in charge could not resist. He generously allowed me to accompany him on a one-hour training flight over Giza.

I was able to take a few shots of the Sphinx and the pyramids of Khufu, Khephren, and Menkaure. But the time of day was all wrong for aerials. It was noon, and the heat of the desert rose as high as the pyramids, creating a photographic nightmare of high-keyed light and lack of contrast. Fortunately, as I subsequently found out, fate had played a sympathetic hand. Not only had I met the right person at the right moment, for this flight was highly unusual (and quite against the rules), but when I returned to the States, I was ecstatic to find that the Sphinx and pyramids appeared in the photographs as delicate ghosts emerging from a mysterious desert landscape. At that moment, I knew that I would have to return to Egypt.

Several years later, when I was invited to give a slide lecture at the National Arts Club in New York City, an archaeologist from Boston University saw the few Egyptian images in my presentation and commented on how rare they were. In his experience, planes and permissions to photograph in Egypt were almost impossible to obtain. He was delighted with the quality and detail of the photographs and encouraged me to continue my Egyptian work. I had just finished a large documentation on Peru and was ready for a new project. This time, after several months' research, I sought the necessary permissions in advance and thoroughly planned my Egyptian itinerary. I approached the Egyptian embassy in Washington and was informed that I first needed official clearance from the Ministry of Defense — no easy task, especially for a woman! After writing many letters to Cairo and receiving no response, I gathered up my cameras in October 1992 and boarded a plane for Egypt to see what could be done on the spot.

It was not a good time to go. Newspapers were full of reports of fundamentalist disruptions in Cairo and along the Nile — my very destinations — and I was quite apprehensive on arrival. I phoned my old acquaintance the general, only to learn of his upcoming retirement. He remained supportive of my project, however, and managed to pull previously untugged official strings to arrange permissions for my flight from Cairo to Abu Simbel.

The flight proved to be a nerve-racking mission. From the start, the little Cessna 172, rocked by spiraling heat from the desert, did not respond well to the rolling turbulence. Aviation fuel became an acute problem. It was not possible to land and refuel except at a few scattered designated airports because of persistent terrorist activity along the Nile. At one point the pilot pointed the aircraft toward Mecca and handed me the controls while he prayed fervently. His cool military facade began to break down, and he did not respond well to my suggestions. My steadfastness needled him. When we came to a site to be photographed, he would barely circle once or twice before hurrying off to the next location. I was getting my shots but had little chance for backup. I could only hope that experience would carry the day. Still, as the plane rattled its way over the Nile, the sights below were glorious. The pyramids seemed symbiotic with the sand. Stark white tombs honeycombed the landscape. Magnificent skeleton-like temples punctuated villages and towns. It became increasingly obvious that the pilot wanted to terminate the flight. When we finally landed at Luxor, he refused to go on, and my dream of completing the project at Abu Simbel came to an abrupt halt. Our return to Giza allotted no time to photography. I then knew that in order to finish my quest I would have to withstand a bureaucratic quagmire of paperwork and approvals.

Indeed, my final trip to Egypt in 1993 proved to be the most difficult. I had to procure five different clearances from various bureaus of the Ministry of Defense, including a thorough personal clearance to determine that I was not a spy or saboteur. Even so, an intelligence person stayed with me on all flights to ensure that I did not disclose military sites. My film was collected after each flight and further scrutinized. On the ground, this man served as my protector. The tight security measures were not unreasonable. Moslem fundamentalists were threatening tourists. I had to worry about my safety on the ground as well as in the air.

During the first month in Cairo, while clearances were being issued, I tried to charter a plane. A prominent professor became interested in my project and, as a result, I was introduced to the owner of a civil aviation company, who made it clear to me that my only recourse was to use a military helicopter for my flights. He could arrange for the aircraft if permissions were granted. While I was thrilled finally to have flight at my fingertips, I was alarmed because clearly the military planes were potential targets of the terrorists. Every day I was told I could fly tomorrow, *"inshallah!"* (God willing!). But God did not seem to be willing. I passed the time visiting many sites on the ground. I even rode a horse out in the desert and meditated in the temples and by the pyramids. Finally, I traveled overland to Luxor to get my helicopter only to be met with further delays instigated by bureaucratic confusion between the local military commander and my assigned intelligence man.

One evening I couldn't sleep, so I slipped out for a walk through the great temple at Luxor. Alone, and by now very discouraged, I walked among the huge statues of Ramesses II, and asked myself why I was being tested to such an extent. The answer I received was that this was a lesson in patience, as well as one of detachment; I had to learn to let go and, if necessary, accept the unacceptable. "God willing," the trip would work out. And if not . . . ? Fortunately, I never had to face that answer. Because, the next day, the helicopter was available.

It was a remarkable journey. Suspended in space in an old Russian helicopter with a gunman's belt around my body, I flew over the solemn expanse of the Valley of the Kings and continued up the Nile, finally reaching Abu Simbel. Here, the light was glorious. The great stone temples radiated. Shadows flanked and outlined their breadth. The waters of Lake Nasser, which had covered many nearby monuments, nearly touched the temples' gates.

Monuments are meant to be testimonies to permanence. Yet, ruins show us the nature of impermanence, which is something most humans fear because it reminds us of our mortality. The ancient Egyptians, like us, did not want to let go of life. This obsession with life drove them to explore the possibilities of death. Life, like the Nile, became the blood of continuance. Life and death became halves of a whole. Although monuments are imperfect examples of permanence, they remain the cornerstones of history.

There is a saying in Egypt: "When you drink water from the Nile you will always return." Every time I think of my experiences there and look at my photographs, my spirit returns to their source. I'm uplifted, and again I'm flying under the aegis of Isis, soaring above the antiquities of the Nile.

BIBLIOGRAPHY

Photographic Books and CD-ROM

Markings: Aerial Views of Sacred Landscapes, Aperture, Inc., New York, 1986

The Sacred & Secular: A Decade of Aerial Photography, International Center of Photography, New York, 1990

Planet Peru: An Aerial Journey Through a Timeless Land, Aperture, Inc., New York, 1991

Vue d'Oiseau, La Mission Photographique Transmanche, Centre Régional de la Photographie, Douchy, France, 1996

Sacred and Secular: The Aerial Photography of Marilyn Bridges, CD-ROM, The Voyager Company, New York, 1996

Earth Signs, Aperture, Inc., New York, Spring, 1997

Selected Public Collections

American Museum of Natural History, New York
Bibliothèque Nationale, Paris
Canadian Centre for Architecture, Montreal
Center for Creative Photography, University of Arizona, Tucson
Cincinnati Art Museum
Colgate University, Hamilton, New York
Fondation Vincent van Gogh, Arles, France
Hellenic Centre of Photography, Athens, Greece
High Museum of Art, Atlanta
International Center of Photography, New York
International Museum of Photography at George Eastman House, Rochester, New York
Israel Museum, Jerusalem
Library of Congress, Washington, D.C.
Los Angeles County Museum of Art
Metropolitan Museum of Art, New York
Musée de la Photographie, Charleroi, Belgium
Museum of Art, University of Oklahoma, Norman
Museum of the American Indian, New York
Museum of the City of New York
Museum of Fine Arts, Houston
Museum of Modern Art, New York
Museum of Fine Arts, Santa Fe
National Gallery of Canada, Ottawa
National Museum of Anthropology, Lima, Peru
National Museum of Modern Art, Porto, Portugal
Nevada Museum of Art, Reno
North Dakota Museum of Art, Grand Forks
Philadelphia Museum of Art
Royal Commission on Historical Monuments, London
Salt River Project, Phoenix, Arizona
University of Nebraska, Lincoln

Selected Solo Exhibitions

1996 Centre Régional de la Photographie, Nord Pas-de-Calais, Douchy, France
Jacksonville Museum of Contemporary Art, Jacksonville, Florida
Field Museum of Natural History, Chicago

1995 American Museum of Natural History, New York
Foto Mässan, Göteborg, Sweden
Michael C. Carlos Museum, Emory University, Atlanta
Royal Ontario Museum, Toronto, Canada

1994 Palmer Museum of Art, Pennsylvania State University, University Park
Carnegie Museum of Natural History, Pittsburgh
Cincinnati Museum of Natural History

1993 Museum of Art, Duke University, Durham, North Carolina
Etherton Gallery, Tucson, Arizona
Louisiana Arts & Science Center, Baton Rouge

1992 Kansas City Museum, Kansas City, Missouri
Picker Art Gallery, Colgate University, Hamilton, New York
VIII Mes de la Fotografía, Iberoamerica, Casa Colón, Huelva, Spain

1991 Mairie de Mérignac, Fondation Charles Cante, Mérignac, France
Musée Française de la Photographie, Bièvres, France
Museum of Art & Archaeology, University of Missouri, Columbia
Museum of Science & Industry, Chicago

1990 International Center of Photography, New York
Centro de Estudos de Fotografia, Coimbra, Portugal
Gibbes Art Museum, Charleston, South Carolina
Dallas Art Institute
XXIème Rencontres Internationales de la Photographie, Arles, France
Houston Museum of Natural Science

1989 Palm Springs Desert Museum, Palm Springs, California
Museum of Revolution, Beijing, China
Municipalidad de Miraflores, Lima, Peru
1988 Sheldon Swope Art Museum, Terre Haute, Indiana
The Photographers' Gallery, London
1987 Canton Art Institute, Canton, Ohio
Tampa Museum of Art, Tampa, Florida
International Museum of Photography at George Eastman House, Rochester, New York
Burden Gallery, New York
1986 Adler Planetarium, Chicago
Lowe Art Gallery, Syracuse University, Syracuse, New York
Wilderness Park Museum, El Paso, Texas
1985 Hunter Museum of Art, Chattanooga, Tennessee
Edwin A. Ulrich Museum of Art, Wichita State University, Wichita, Kansas
Sheldon Memorial Art Gallery, University of Nebraska, Lincoln
1984 Smithsonian Institution, Washington, D.C.
Foto Biennale, Enschede, The Netherlands
1983 Tucson Museum of Art, Tucson, Arizonia
New York Academy of Sciences, New York
Glenbow Museum, Calgary, Canada
1982 Galeriegesellschaft, Berlin, West Germany
Robert Klein Gallery, Boston
Center for Inter-American Relations, New York
1981 Blue Sky Gallery, Portland, Oregon

Selected Group Exhibitions

1995 Museum of Contemporary Photography, Chicago
Museum of Modern Art, New York
1993 Musée des Beaux Arts, Reims, France
Natuurmuseum, Rotterdam, The Netherlands
Museo de Arte Contemporano Internacional Rufino Tamayo, Mexico City
Museum of Modern Art, New York
1992 High Museum of Art, Atlanta
University of Amsterdam, The Netherlands
Art Institute of Chicago
Palais de Tokyo, Paris
1991 Lieberman & Saul Gallery, New York
Catherine Edelman Gallery, Chicago
1990 Museum of Fine Arts, Houston
1989 University of Oklahoma Museum of Art, Norman
Philadelphia Museum of Art
1988 Harvard School of Design, Cambridge, Massachusetts
Aspen Art Museum, Aspen, Colorado
1987 Norton Gallery, West Palm Beach, Florida
Museum of Art and History, San Juan, Puerto Rico
Contemporary Arts Center, Cincinnati
Utah Museum of Fine Arts, Salt Lake City
Baltimore Museum of Art
Triennale, Charleroi, Belgium
Tweed Museum, Duluth, Minnesota
1985 Musée des Beaux Arts, Tours, France
São Paulo Bienal, São Paulo, Brazil
Addison Gallery of American Arts, Andover, Massachusetts
Catskill Center for Photography, Woodstock, New York
1984 Bibliothèque Nationale, Paris
1983 Friends of Photography, Carmel, California
1982 Museum of Modern Art, New York
Seibu Museum of Art, Tokyo
University of Hawaii, Honolulu
American Museum of Natural History, New York
1981 National Museum of Modern Art, Porto, Portugal
MFA Gallery, Rochester Institute of Technology, Rochester, New York
1980 Memorial Art Gallery, Rochester, New York

Awards, Honors and Accredidations

Guggenheim Fellowship 1982
CAPS Grant 1983
NEA Grant 1984
Fulbright Grant 1988–9
Makedonas Kostas Award (Greece) 1989
Elected fellow of The Explorers Club 1988
Pilot, single and multi-engine land and sea aircraft